OF MONODIES AND HOMOPHONY

EDRIC MESMER

Outriders Poetry Project
Buffalo, NY
2015

OF MONODIES AND HOMOPHONY is the competition winner for the 2014 "Outriders Selection," selected by Jerry McGuire.

ISBN13: 978-0-9910724-2-2

ISBN10: 0991072421

Some works in this book have been previously published as follows: "Dorsality" in *Aufgabe 12*; "Due Fault" in *Cordite Poetry Review*; "Delphine" in *Landscapes: Journal of the International Centre for Landscape and Language*; "Aloud" in *Yellow Field* 3; "Were I They" in *Brigid's Fire*, vol. 1; and "58" [from "Pyramidal"] in *Vanitas 5*. "A khimera" and "Flagging legends" appear in Pat Tansey's anthology *A Celebration of Western New York Poets*.

"Evidence Gathers," "In Supporting Arcades," "Intaking Water," and "For Islet" first appeared in the chapbook *Intaking Water* (Orkneys: Seapressed/ meta, 2011), with thanks to publisher and friend Mark Dickinson.

Cover art: "Collective Move" (2004) by Monica Angle, courtesy of the artist.

Cover layout: Judy Vasseur

Contents

for Brian

and

in memory of Norma

OF MONODIES AND HOMOPHONY

10 Kinds of Quiet

anyone who says Foucauldian
who had wanted to say Foucault
and then Foucauldian said to have
said "d" instead of not saying "t"

saying and not saying "t"
saying and saying
and writing not
"d" (and this was palatal)

that is to say palatable by
etymologic corollary
for sake of saying or
writing what's unsayable

what do you say to antithesis?
thesis: forsook graphology
hypothesis: that in varieties of silence
autonomy may be nascent

autonomy, the dream world
between the bridge and colossus
between, singly, a rephrasing of question
. . . and Fascism of colossus

what of "d"s and "t"s *en palette?*
what of bridges uttered in dot matrix?
author: no paradigm was uncleft by
this reference

no authorial avalanche was resultant from
said reference, not
see reference, written:
"hypothesis," whereas the ticket read

"name." name
name a last chance at admittance.
admit it—you had had it with
permissions—admit once:

you had been silently reading,
nearly forgetting that
who hath forgotten Polonium
hath also Germanium forgot.

anybody? any-
body an antibody;
a thesis in antithesis;
a new kind of Valentine: I hate you.

antipathy temporal anyway.

antipathy a template,

bridging colossus . . .

no paradigms inured in this minute engendering.

enter gender then and you tweak terms

you—or no one—tweak terms to your affections

your affectations

Olde Logick

ponder fixity

ponder saying nothing

like gravel on lilies

like gravel beneath barefoot and tire tread

all the while you had been looking at paradigms

inclusive of sexed diffidence

all the while I had been silent, except

now I long feel I've been screaming

CASCADENCE

    relational
        to each neighbor here-
            by by sheer balcony alift,
fleet-like in cardinality
        —for from east one cannot see
            one's western neighbor who
may have it in for me,
        for the one strewing honeyed
            petals over the shared car-
lot, like Carlotta, despi-
        sing Daaé her sunrise slot—all
            tiered, and below the Dana-
ides are watering win-
        dow boxes of hyacinth, just as
            Danaë might wring out
her hair, drenched with
        Prell-for-non-blondes, mean-
            while the Graeae flatter
me with troubadour
        hours, and I mark striations
            in the days' wendings—
that hour said to shine
        green like a flash in the pan,
            as the lake pushes to ex-
tremity its oblong cir-
        cumference in preferring my
            railed ledge to its edgily
lacking salinity, and for
        once, from below, someone
            might catapult my way
a timepiece to keep
        better by my biding this ivy
            draping, *Digitalis digitalia*
over a handrail, even
        though from here even the
            elevator won't hold for
center, and the moon

moves through shale-like
clouds, how someone has
left plastine trails a-
dangle from one infringe-
ment upon another—all
the ways we know
ourselves, polarized, like
how the 8th becomes the 7th be-
comes the 6th floor
balcony, zip-line-fashion, the
latex paint wavering away
from cement canopies,
detritus of underwaves, our
own echoes, stand-in *sotto voce*
in these coves, cover
from the open architecture
of the new code, a zone from
which one cannot re-
treat so neighborly, on January
balconies or from balconies
Augustan...the lobbed
lobsterlike adding patina to the
baby blue (not-so-new) brick
edifices, these sheltered
economies, where mermaids a-
wash in swift storms off
Erie recompose dirges
I rest here from mythology,
anxious that pale azure will
temper the way I feel
at great heights—fate lights
the vantage of vanishing we've
yet to know as collapse
in swathes of billowing gar-
ment, like a tunic found in
an eddy of cross breeze,
indicative of some basking un-
iformly unworn since
Tiresias.

In Sequestration's Milieu, Un-

heralded
        by the heavy
machinery we layer—
we lay our pas-

sions over—
that the machinations of be
theses in-

ventoried in-
novatively when
apropos of machinists' limn

A tangent
a chord—accord
to some circle(s) to

yet be described
in ascription
per se

forerunners "en
Mer," such as lines
of discord

record (*mar*

jour) these

Cardigan shores

weary

of wayfarer's

welcome—

the earlied glades

a sextant unassail-

able, roves

BATHYMETRY

On bank holidays

you'd think boys could

be as nymphs

and a three-quarter

bath pajamas...

The found poem crinkles and cleanly

dissolves like a spined book left

splayed near the fire lad-

der, not before de-

crypting

War'og
scored a m—
jor Anthony Du
and 4, and the
twentieth hole
before he elim-
Bishop the a
-ampion
The

choice between hand soap and face soap

the ordering of racked towels

de omnibus rebus, et quibusdam aliis—

sauve qui peut—

1A   B   C   D   E   F

2

3

4

5

6

                    dross across

            the timber

      from a half-trunk

        through with wire

   where cords din

         in static rinse

    diurnally over pavement some un

       -etched cenotaph

          lichen dichten

          wee genii

        of ennui

A KHIMERA

In his dream
the vocabulary may begin:

[Cyrillic **D**]
О{
91

Though she is muted
he is reading her face;

though he cannot listen
she is thoroughly cursory.

You can take: take Stravinsky.

Lapped
as the conch

is the French
horn's bell;

tonight
empyrean

symbols
what you will:

analysis

in excess

horny toad.

Of a sudden
there is orchestra—

weren't allover these chambers
alchemic?

4'33" rhyming
meaning melodious.

[A saint's]

apostrophe{

the <u>date</u>?

Tablature
scant tableaux,

the eye on
its nightstand ev-

anesces; nor
composure or

carbon makes them one: rosette.

Defiling phylum
in whose image

your arm foregrounds
mine "and thou art borne."

EVIDENCE GATHERS

You have been looking at looking

as privacy awaits guests

a new kind of dysphoria

. . . and the system no longer distends as from center, an

allocating heteronomy—

a page enters

—is sent away...

Meant to be opened, locked boxes.

Consider that the garment is your image

an hitherto sex

clothing of water

An eminent domain of knowledge, modestly

retrofit.

On the dark side of a broadening square

these coexistents—

the circular process (and) gathering normality

(gazing upon one's own gaze)

evinces this gathering

as does that   the felling tree   androgyny

—perhaps you would, an episteme, hazard?

observing, removed, the beauty of the gathering bathers

A Genealogy   erecting felled trees

and additive of occluded view . . .

"I'm not an oboist, but"

The Swans, The Swans!

—their appetites

AFTER MONICA ANGLE'S *DIVISION OF WATER*

for Jo Cook

As we leave now the shore of the textual

As we leav—

        Now the shore of

                —he textual

                An ibis unis

                 led

As we leav   *(unisled)*   'he textual

As we leaf   or

        cease to leaf

we leave   the shore off

        this textuality

As we leaf now   his textuality

    now the shore of the

textual

          As we leave

"the dead/ly hand / of a radium clock"

as with a sheaf of text left

verso

As now the shore   we make left the recto

And we leaving text   now shored in how

is the sign of our complacency

—sheave apparel—

As we are but the psi to the trident

As the shore   now and then   then trident

mooring in a textuality of the now

Ψ

As a sawyer

snores the river that enters the lake

in eventuality

within its own eventuality

17

a bower

with the hoar of the textual on worn sleeves green...

As we leave off now

        our costumes

As we leave off now

        our costumes

            and slip within the skeins

      of cataract

And as ours are also signs

of our own cohort

          sinusoidal

        and without harmonic—

not sacerdotal

        save for antidotal

               $\forall$ *TABLE*

          of the

      NTENT

      legibly become

                 a Rubicon—

this lexicon—

         as how a glyph now for our mutual friend

                Hieronymous

is

become

eponymous

FLAGGING LEGENDS

From my bathroom win-
              dow a mosaic fount mud-sunk...

But from my bedroom   the nightshade
            of a stop sign flung over the fire hydrant

                              Sinews of arrest bequeath

            the fixed shade of diurnal rapture
                      In yards concretized

      pools that fall from a trampoline's surface

                      in the locution of fortune
            quincunx

The Doubting Optimist
              in a window for modernity

            daringly faces away
                  as the Pleiad turned   ever after Troy

Even she counters counte-
              nance never so much as by archetype

                              Rested thereon
        "something represented or indicated in a work of art"

              However she hopes she is wrong

IN SUPPORTING ARCADES

Also: the turn away from
coterie; the wan-slung
gallery, with whale's bones
made apothecary's
curio—
       Grant trace
obligatory lime and fossil
soldiering artifice read
for society lest

a stitch of crossbow cross
the flagstones' manse
and tell the house
elect that a-
       kin to purvey's
dicta
       there must be marvel's quota
fond of fawn and copse
              and nymphine issue
      —none recital

nor vogue for notion

in contemporaneity

heeds a shelf

        in atrophy

heads a deadening

          citation

as gesturative palm gone impassionedly to forehead

to rarity of brow

seated against an opprobrium on brow

where, seated, grapes of toe emerge

from marble

         thrown as dice thrown

Elgin—globular

        foot of Sappho

WERE I THEY

            cottoning sunshine under the same sign as James Dean,

    or,

"on the minus side,"

           seen nonaggressively, "cocked in the snaky S-curve usually

    reserved" beyond

the soft and ripped jersey of identity, subordinating to poster

iconography,

and, were I they, agora-sexuality—would orient taboo, and passively embed culture

    in a fulcrum of self-worth and gazing pools

                 temporizing, as is the visual talisman,

          when clutched to—as to naked cloth—

    by scions at odds with Atropos' favor—

were I they

were I they

both ways and all ways making voyeuses of stimuli

as the crocus-traced narcissus, hanging aesthetics within quotation,

"were I they"

were it not for whetted Ganymede,

conceived of in the visceral pliancy of orgiastic thought—

the conference and the audience

androgynizing in the agency of rough Freuding, not even;

the unified reader speaks don't against the truck of referenced eyes

gazing (were I they) upon great mummers occluded in cacophony

tailoring—in all ways—how

a genealogy finds relevance.

ALOUD

Consensus clouds

houses caucus

Datum

cum

Brother-

hood in lavishly

patronized piss-rooms

panhandling the insignificant tributes

to the choicest lacks thereof

retrieved from hiving cellars

sheaves a barrier Lo

salient misnomers

in standard American usage

a calculus non sequitur

on catgut in academe's

groove bohème's trove

the cuttlefish angelic "not

a fan of gender"

nor an anemone

nor lilied rug omni-

relevant to ponder "sea-sound-

empty-full"

a rhetorical [de] instruction

empiric vox riddles

in the economy of dyads

        Some isle arks oar to too

        and cede sells fate

        in jewels sensor freeze

        Phased gilt

needs nocturne to whom actuality ac-

cordions

in toneless tones repentant

"one must be worthy" as

        Sum I'll arcs ore tutu

        and seed cells fête

        in joules censor frieze

        Fazed guilt

kneads knowledges

mineral spilled

past cascading subjects un-

toward grotto blue

DORSALITY

for Mark Dickinson*'s "*not-yet*"*

sun + wind
water + sand
—Rhoda Rosenfeld

and the mythos riddled with clap
of waved thunder, banter at Atlantis
the sand-cast whatnot of court rot
taken to forge : : pig-iron
volcanic distants—
        wraith as rite

as drawn from Circe, her head
band and unwind mien's shell
little cockles till the frags
read ECRIC and call this hearsay
the aural on the back of the grap
heme stream gulfed

        gleam and who aren't
thou sovereign to?
                as
        islet
        is-let

I let go as sloe floes &

        I AM CONTINENT

27

arcades opaqued

like masts, and wade   *"plash*

plash"

pelagic graphs

—sand dried on the abdomen

(Artemis's, or of Hermes)

—orifice to orifice—

the flex-breath   *omphalos*
where once the willow bent
to fresh vein, divining...

and not changeling—
fed the codpiece
harlequin's
lumberjack seat flap
not—

...kno...

no

hero-

worn

shore

an out-

line div-

ides as by

scion

        of the washed-up

                sea-sputtered utterer

                        raiment-draped

                        no longer

drawn

and un-

quartered

stylus

marking   mark

making   scepter when

                   thrown

                   to the ashen

                   sands

& for

all

this

you trade a

jagged helmet

haircut

of blunt

wet fringe

and ton-

sure not

yet and

yet not

a moon

at noon

—is the conquering between the

text in sand and sand or

and sea or between

wind sand

and sea

?...the sightless text

blight-textured

in the wet maw

visuality

an out-

line yet

not an

antihero

    merely

the dorsal

[*sun + wind*
water + sand]

    The wrest of land from sea is seldom

    tranquil even the piling plankton

    coral reef and bower barrier

    or the slaking bridge iron

    tendrils to their bases taut

    columns calumny jets

Siphonal the sheer torsion ce-

phalic H.D.'s gonad-like jelly-

fish tentacles cap madder than

raddle in the cyan incom-

mensurate

canopy where [ecriC] like rubbish eddies

a mirror for Circe to call in circum-

ference without

center—as—as into port—enters

æquum noctis

braiding the land-limit-libido with reddened-copper

of the not-yet oxidized

redux found in pre-aqua

kenning

keening

LARGESSE

Miniatures, the adolescent mars,
now before the dawn dries, the tread
grooves, or the bow saws
you would like I should want to be, but I've never save
for the breaking treble;
you would need I should,
desirous, and
clutching the breakneck border,
the undisclosed body
cunning dissed and open

I've not been
breaking but breaking
over eras, voids, contrapositiv-
ism, as writ...The wind is becoming
the stone it once thought to erode—
Patinæ ADOREMVS *dormir*. Mold
sleeps painted in the hue of the grot-
to, to become the grate through which time re-
vises the near-archa-
ic torsion, the image of Venn, our vet-
ting, ambivalents; n/or is the unicorn
"just a unicorn"
I fathom by

your head, your mask

your worshipper and your Sumer

your eucharistic dove, your Georgia M. G. Forman

your altar and

your panel

your granite Brahma, your Mrs. Seymour Knox, Sr.

your Artemis

> and your stag

your 1937

your pur-

chase, your earthenware

and your prancing horse, your King, Benin

and your bequest, your seated poet, your

Gabon, your alabaster

your Flemish Christ, your "one of about 600 surviving examples in the world"

your Madonna and Child del-

> la Italia

your 13th c. and your 1953,

your Rhenish or the Netherlands, your

terra cotta lamentation, your limestone jar

your Zuñi and your polychrome

your sixth dynasty

your tassels

your anthro and POMOrphism

your aqua-fine dragon and your effigy; even now,

Antique Hairdo with Salt and Pepper, echoes

say hiddenness wont to later murmur hidden...

Not necessarily not necessary

this small inheritance.

                      Cyano-

type, you are that juggling what

with "agreeable recreation to the eye" Pisces fucks:

head-to-tail with gryphons

        constellatory, the starry-

        footed up to their a[r]ses

        in chain-link diadem; fishes

        suspend, in ibidem—

            ...Doppelgangers are kis-

            sing in this Ganges.

OF AN AGE

> Shading the fin
de siècle, as to lave
> a rib, as to score
parchment in in-
> finite sinew. Mind
in turn, centri-
> fugal sung;
rut and gauge; of an
> age bygone: instructional.
Antiquity, your ablution
> is subaqueous, asking a
chalice when cup suf-
> fices "verbatim and literatim"—ere
in compendium
> redolently il-
lumined...Sibilants
> ripple amber...disagree-
ing as to the end of image where-
> in "(the concept of the line is not employed)"
choir and quire
> are homonyms and
synonymous—no chance.

FOR ISLET

P. Chamoiseau + D.H. Lawrence

1.

Verge would be our vantage, purview's sake, because we love to be alone and found, and because founding is to have once been lost. And loss we'd not forsaken.

2.

Disbelief of evening, maybe, a curvilinear night no less cyclic than cicada's crick. For endlessness a want of door, perhaps, and windows all on moorings; for the cabinetry to be, to be creatures of tendency.

3.

In looking we'd seemed not to find scar of evidence, nook of absence. Simply looking over compiled—looking over eyes of posture—looking over looking.

4.

Yet when the rapt and half-ensconced lolled in tide's possession, we went as weeks back into ritual, to self-same and in doctrine. We passed for vision. Built harbors filled in in inlets rhythm, and ducked before the ocular ways of ethereal either.

5.

Suddenly were startling verges met, for sake of kindling, kith and autumn. Our own rain barrels were sure to augur, coat and sugar, recoil a little. For then we knew lake's life was ours. Dropped hidden.

6.

A passage ran the thicket, thickset. What we weren't recording had yet no measure. Document; pleasure. Sought in heather the horns of minotaur and torn the weeds from lilies.

7.

I entered shrewdly, cornerstone laid, in orbit. Dusk now was soundness. Isles would much less catch

8.

in the riverine labyrinth nought, catchy as the bass is caught.

9.

A magnet snagged in the quarry, where we went to be ourselves, and hide what little else is sacred in the day-tinged optics. I saw a bull-shaped estuary. I saw a target seeing me. I saw a sea as supreme act of antecedent islanding, and willed it be.

10.

Repeat after [sea]:

> "Know."

> "Yeah."

> "If, say," "'If so.'"

And cattails bent to catfish gills, silence pursed—the voice a log in damming.

11.

On the far side, table...

The dream is cottoning the corners of the sentence, this emittance; a first room in our sequestering sonar.

12.

Listening to "so tenderly, so tenderly" listening to your bosky voice "so tenderly" round the isle.

13.

But as to circumvent, the sea arch perch, the radial view, built into the tide-reef-tide articulable, in counterbalances we dare not secret here. Here, where, here-where we are foxy.

14.

Repeat after [cornerstone], an optic estuary targeted.

I looked over my shoulder, and an evening disbelieved; I mean: I looked over your

shoulder and the endless cycle fraught so

15.

lee and bow the littoral non-diurnal.

16.

And thus it seemed to we that landscape was cessation conducted, and us this

wondrous aquiver mar in mirage thinking, probably—don't you? Doomed to.

Overlooking.

and "wear a thin gold bracelet above my left elbow…"
A name for story begun in quotes; in diffidence,
representation: "*Je ne Parle pas Français.*"

Begun foreignness, in col-
loquial seme, lost to italics, to quote,
the sensuous type of speech,

the phenotypic thought,
perhaps, the genotype
of print; tones hewn

alike: composing sticks
some loss ruled to a
grammar, a handbook

plugging away in the
parlay. Did I say
that? "A whole

nother thing," another
thing itself. And what of that
cold gold band, the ellipsis?

Ellipsis above devil's
elbow, the wrong-handedness
clasped in wrong-headedness—

head in hands. "Whose
head in hands *of whom*—?" His—
handheld when, emptied of bracelet,

held instead, to the body,
the body of work, his corpus.
You had known it was he,

known him, what it was for him
to be without these institutions, the
matrices of patriarchy...

But what of vein, of ore,
of the tanned arm, or of
pallor? you who have

slated him to this isle, into exile.

Sirens are naming

—cockle

—polestar

—*S.S. Ganymede*

the one that went down

went down discharging

100,000   Ganynauts

into troves

repository

the carte none

too blanche

rest here'in

cove

cradle

'd elbow

dear

del blanco

INTAKING WATER

1

"Make it sound sexy—who cares?" Hubris
Management cares...the gullhead rolled in
under crest, and your retreat
to breast-level, belt below surface

Again the interests of repository
against the interest of repository—
wave-like vocables in an irrevocable
lake

2

A matter of knot,
desirous of swimmer...You're unit
of standard un-
equivocal—no

pedagogue,
mouth agog,
ho-humming the
hole of meaning

3

Liminal me, on my shore, e-
ither America, as we say, or
Canada (still America) though
what's that red-tiled islet

circulating on the lip of int'l waters?
It corresponds or makes line
toward the hydroplant state-
side—pixie kissing tritons

4

"There are two types of people in this world, my type of people
and assholes," but there're only
three colors in the additive perception line-making
making line of ir-

regularities—red, blue, green—"Beneath
the ochre syllables other
syllables," the lossy hide
of lyric in lossless tide

5

Taking a load off, cannily,
pants cuffed, hiked up over knees
with waist flown with the stream-
line, buckling in unbridled breeze

All tail in a peg-legged nar-
rative, or jeans, wet and sandy
as caked flank—a variorum
of species, the two-tailed you turn forked tongue to

6

I wanna throw down some
terms in the seamy throes
of continuous yet indefinite re-
presentation

In the studied contrast of level
tones, the choreographic bevel
—I want this cyclical hovel
to be my foam, form, nonce, and novel

7

Recall the red-tiled intake problematic
gulps a fluid ounce of
steam off seaweed-draped fog-
horn carving oar...

No way to fashion quay
of theoretic sashay along a quay
only for he am I stationed at quay's
end—a Speedo is made for speed

8

What the fuck am I doing, subject
to the net and skyline-caught
as by the expert fishmonger
—I must be on the nether

side, dependent on horizon,
lest I'm underwater, threading a
quadrant not yet disciplined, any
way, disciple to your tread

A QUOTIENT OF INTENTION

> *Campbell's Tomato Soup*
> *cream of tomato soup*
> *beef and barley*

1

Countering functionlessness

by the pamphlet for the union in

blue hues as by Gray

As placed upon a table by Eileen Gray

as on a table by Gray, as by Delaunay

all in blues of Coltrane

This blueprint sent to the printer's, then

freelanced to a subsidiary in France,

reread in-house by the apprentice

2

What the apprentice intended with

white-out as getting back his

blue period

So patrons lost and sought

in the onslaught of architectural

belles lettres spoke little of Triolet

As origin as well as originator

authenticates an *a priori* labeling

-what tautology can and can't

3

Can: exemplars wont and oppositional

Can't: by label or by house of style

Can-and-can't: blueprint quintessent

In "adjudication between these two theories"

(begin quote, begin single-quote, theory qua

theory, end single-quote, end quote

(reverse quotes variant in original)) As to account

for apprenticeship's usurping sanctioned voice, or

a quality of vellum chosen for a standard

4

As a house dispersed, "archive in" flotsam

a style emergent, archive in jetsam—

an insular margin

A marginal anomaly

in an edition in French (translated) from an

handwritten folio lent the apprentice-cum-impresario

Appearing as newly warmed Norton ab-
ridgement illustriously lacking
algorithmic polemic

5
Watery light on the undersides of branch
branch of the incorporated refinery
Lumber Tycoon To Visit Mills

A foreign manifesto, in the words
of a correspondent, since expatriated, to
be published, copyright 1914

Implicitly ghosting
virtual industries
by the rippling pastoral

6
As, India paper, bound
at rear of travelogue, map-
ping *laissez-faire*, is

Stamped for due-date to, em-
bossed by institution from, to
whom the castigator

belongs, and from

whom cascades as many questions

chased as chaste

7

Blue prompt

for a book of yellowing—blues

for a *Yellow Book* read or un-

By this coterie, beside censure

"can" and "can't" functioning

minus lumberer

By tawny sinew, barely

changed of shift, of

changedness, of a garde

Pyramidal

after Vertov

and without interstices

without scenario
with total separation from
the language of theatre

a portrait for two cameras
and the chandelier the metro-
nome for silence

the campanile and the clavicle
"a sphere of soldered nails"
unlike the clasps of brassieres un-

like shivering chemises yet
to torso, awash in nakedness
the hydrants these mums focus

"58"

a great ass-shot of parasol, wherewithal

the britches of carriages

and milliners' creations the

pucks of ponies clubs

          in stile

one plus two-halves

      (*al*most two...)

thus a film of

the cutting room starlet

pinning a grimace

under over-

cast

hands—hers lacquered

        in opacity

so with mesmerism

"Hello?" "Hello."
and next of kin

as was pyramidal
shorn and threaded, this image

of near-antonyms blathering—
of Doppler, reverb

perambulating permanencies of bell
O, homochronic zeitgeist!

in translucence
rain-rinsed glass

an ember

embers, love
remembered, re-
routed, in water
a flag of surrender

hovering between a pulley
in silence and black and white

whose
very ism, whenever
were titans

in heroic lit discourse

spilled bottled water
tween

DUE FAULT

after Loy

i

in pound psalt
aspersions
as pert
as
locutions—

a balm for the faux prince
confused for
for cannon fodder
with a dauphin daft
as can be had,

greasing an Occitan
flute of meth au
gratin,
flagellum off
curdled champagne—

he sees among the orgiastic
Rorschachs of brass an
ampersand in un-
common continuum,
labeled libelously bile

ii

fallen headlong into crater—
yeasty chaser of chancre—
under the watchful eye
of that traitorous
Cyclops, moon:

tells you which song,
nearing nadir, to
ring unto the loin-slung
day—making the red
rock dust Equator

a season in yellow—
a slow drawl on elbow,
withholding
of candlewick for the en-
flame of tonsil—

hold tight, Night:
your spates are purloined,
gossamer gone with talcum to
copulate in the cupola
of a nucleotide

iii

due fault for such trellis! led up
flights of chalky
scaffold on-
ly to meander
the lattice-patter of a slumberer

—a milk-moustache
of thrush
in the piss-venetian air
of morning,
frosting your matted hair...

reaching for mnemonic som-
nambulance—reach for your-
self in reek of sleep-
lessness—an Onanist
has firsts and laughs last

...then again, coffee for
your cream; a seam
in the least seemly
of places—must mean we
were allover meant to be seen

iv

make me a doorjamb
in the puerile gatefolds
of Sodom, back arched un-
toward Bethlehem, in
slouch of pasture—

you have a hambone,
I, the ass's jaw,
and our fricatives
and glottal stops
make plosive the logorrhetic...

lean here under the key-
stone Apathy
while marauders nod
to the humorless breeze
moving between the Sphinx' haunches

...you and the doorway and
mystery: one aperture
in the quasi-rapture
of tonight that hath so far
more than pockets, mouths

v

returned to the scene splenetic,
frenzied in its orgy of
still lifes—stunt a common
pose, contrapuntal
to the sensual:

orange rinds in rounds—
milk's pelt; days
glow in the shade
of remembered half-grips
or a chokehold

over the nine-to-five grope
of frigates dumb for a pier
—you've yet a twilit eye-
lid, cancelling the re-
calcitrance of humors /

spread now / the phalanx
of your flank's defense—
there will be no recompense:
the sordid tooth, brush burn, tongue
forked, entendre doubly sore

vi

turned to muted canopies of brick—
(your collar, higher...)
to cellars of shtick—
to the liquorish wrought lines of stencil
the eye twines down...

you've a knack for inter-
continental drift—
fleet way of referencing the sartorial
(with some cheek—)
though the belt slits well still at each cinch...

roll us under the lush
light of irradiant fractal,
of cut glass, cutlass
at arm's length
from this barstool...

dinner now is a minnow of heaven,
a half-hour at matins,
your hand in my mitten...
just as the barkeep sweeps
the dregs of us into taxis

vii

all mango martinis
find the codified esophagi
of night-streets
cobbled—they are clotted
in our most pasteurized vices...

O that Endymion would
shift a hip, let a gasp
pass the
inebriated nimbus of
his blanched shaft—

the tides laugh,
older than prostitution,
given over to
fruition, walking all
cads on leashes Mab's—

and we, excretions,
of the mucused brain re-
arranged in secret passions
no longer, linger-
er, loner

DELPHINE

>*...and seamen invoked her blessing on long voyages...*

i

conch chaise—
the seminal lain upon upon

face—
on long voyages

as on millipedic oars
hangs defeat

dominion wide or
docent deep

ii

fat kid in a fig
leaf, outgrows

leaden kid-
gloves gripping premature-

ly the glissandi
on bastard wings

—he seeks porn-
ography to sublimate

via voyeuristic help-
mate—the distaste-

ful otology of
his mother's spate

for war, rot-
ting fug palate...

iii

for this
an oracle was slain?

sluttish
logorrhea knows

better than to best
the messenger who reads for

Psyche, when
she took to fan-

cy landscape
and drowned in gaseous fracture

all too inky:
a whole well

iv

—morn

finds the pimp out—

the shit the

seagulls squeak upon,

a spit of pier

where overripe ambrosia

adumbrates the

damask lass unasked

to prove her salt

in civic tasks:

the sorting from seed the

husk; rasp

from

memory,

from sham-

poo,

a dram;

and from flagon, as

for Proserpine,

something blue...

v

sing me not

—sing not

Psychology's lyres

are tortoise shelled,

the coxcombs

scrambling into livery—

all lullabies are but song,

and if a gossamer

of egress

should tether to my wayward

ego

let it go, let go

Hermes,

your handheld helix:

suave eloquence; as

Millet's night, turned Van Gogh's...

vi

spheres,
vaguer fancies, love;

trumpet for
a pond—

taken for a sonnet,
lest—les-

ser divinities—
hearth on

vii

in t-shirts concert minstrelsy a
heavenfull's syringe—

for even the simplest reed
proves often

the very flute—
glimpsing

great acts of contrition
gone down with

gravitas,
razor's-edged—not the only face an

ass has—
wherever supple reeds

grasp
as capillary

the cloven chasm where-
in an anemone moans—

viii

o, canal of man-
made

necromancy,
triangulate

this water-
way!

where young tri-
tons pull

with glass-cut
pelvises the

constellatory against
the very sirens

who descry
like their anti-orphic

cousins,
banshees,

fangled dangers of
choral tyranny—

ix

...no choral tyranny

        however

              in oaring

awhile a shore

x

—and what say you to heroes?
gone in to tides

like thunder, their
thighs spanked mercury

—the gorgon's comb
a trove to each—

finding a deity in every minute,
all the mute

suppositions of material
come back from

Poseidon, for a swim,
still unkissed

EDRIC MESMER was born in Buffalo, earned his B.A. from the College of Geneseo, New York, and a Master's degree in Gender, Sexuality and Culture from the University Manchester (England). He returned to the University at Buffalo, where he completed work for an M.A. in Library Science and currently serves Poetry Cataloger to the University at Buffalo's Poetry Collection. Prior to this appointment, he worked on the editorial staff of Scholastic Press, taught at Buffalo State College and D'Youville College, and worked in various bookshops. Currently he curates a series of talks for the Poetry Collection entitled the Center for Marginalia Presents.

Edric Mesmer's poems have appeared in journals and anthologies, including *Infinity's Kitchen*, *Aufgabe*, *Landscapes* (Australia), and *Vanitas*; his critical prose has been featured in *Galatea Resurrects*, *Cordite Review of Poetry*, *Saint Mark's Poetry Project Newsletter*, and *ON: Contemporary Practice*. He has published three chapbooks: *Faun for a noon* (Red Glass Books), *Yrtemmyys* (PressBoardPress), and *Intaking Water* (Seapressed/ meta). Since 2006 he has been editor of *Yellow Edenwald* Field, expanded as *Yellow Field* in 2010, and of a series of small press monographs from the Buffalo Ochre Papers issuing work by, among others, William Sylvester, Norma Kassirer, Donna Wyszomierski, and Marten Clibbens.

The **OUTRIDERS POETRY PROJECT** was founded in 1968 by Doug Eichhorn, Dan Murray, and Max Wickert. With partial support from Poets & Writers and the New York State Council of the Arts, we sponsored numerous readings by poets and fiction writers, both local and national. Since 2009, we have been operating chiefly as a small press, publishing work by writers living in, or significantly associated with, the Buffalo-Niagara region. Submissions for new books, including manuscripts submitted in the annual "Outriders Selection," are considered each year between January 1 and April 15.

For details check our website: *http://www.outriderspoetryproject.com/* or write to: Outriders Poetry Project, 314 Highland Avenue, Buffalo, New York 14222 (tel:716-882-1642; email: *outriderspoetry@me.com*)

Other Outriders Book in Print

Ann Goldsmith, *The Spaces Between Us* (ISBN 0-0981772-0-5; $12.95)

Max Wickert, *Pat Sonnets* (Street Press, 2000; distributed by Outriders; ISBN 0-0935252-55-X, $10.00)

Martin Pops, *Minoxidyl and Other Stories* (ISBN 0-0981772-1-9; $24.95)

Judith Slater, *The Wind Turning Pages* (ISBN 0-0981772-2-1, $12.95)

Max Wickert, *No Cartoons* (ISBN 0-0981772-6-4, $12.95)

Gail Fischer, *Red Ball Jets* (ISBN 0-0984172-4-0, $12.95)

Jeremiah Rush Bowen, *Consolations* (ISBN 0-0981772-5-6. $12.95)

Max Wickert, *All the Weight of the Still Midnight* (ISBN 0-0981772-6-4, $12.95)

Jerry McGuire, *Venus Transit* (ISBN 0-0981772-7-1, $12.95)

Max Wickert (ed.), *An Outriders Anthology: Poetry in Buffalo 1969- 1979 and After* (ISBN 0-098172-8-0 paper, $30; 0-098172-9-9; cloth, $45)

Jacob Schepers, *A Bundle of Careful Compromises* (ISBN 0-991072405; $12.95)

Linda Zisquit, *Return from Elsewhere* (ISBN-0-991072413; $15)